JEAN JONES
v.
KIDS-R-OURS, INC.

Hollace P. Brooks
and Paul Chill
University of Connecticut
School of Law

NATIONAL INSTITUTE FOR TRIAL ADVOCACY

Brooks, Hollace P. and Paul Chill, *Jones v. Kids-R-Ours, Inc.* (NITA, 1995).

ISBN 1-55681-458-5

6/95   4/07

JONES v. KIDS-R-OURS, INC.

CONTENTS

UNITED STATES DISTRICT COURT
DISTRICT OF NITA

JEAN JONES,   :   CIVIL NO. N-93-96369 (ABC)
      Plaintiff,   :

v.   :

KIDS-R-OURS, INC.,   :   SEPTEMBER 15, YR-2
      Defendant   :

COMPLAINT

Introduction

1.   The plaintiff, Jean Jones, brings this action under Title I of the Americans with Disabilities Act, 42 U.S.C. § 12111 et seq., ("ADA"), to redress her unlawful demotion and dismissal from employment by the defendant because of her disability.

Jurisdiction

2.   The court's jurisdiction over this matter is conferred by 42 U.S.C. § 12117 and 28 U.S.C. § 1331.

Parties

3.   The plaintiff, Jean Jones, is a resident of Nita City, Nita. The plaintiff is a person with a disability under the ADA in that she has a physical impairment, epilepsy, that substantially limits one or more of her major life activities.

4.   The defendant, Kids-R-Ours, Inc., is a corporation licensed and existing under the laws of the State of Nita. Upon information and belief, the defendant employs more than 25 persons.

Facts

5.   In July, YR-2, the defendant hired the plaintiff to work as the head teacher in the two year old class at the defendant's Nita City, Nita, day-care center, at an annual salary of $18,000.

6.   At all times after being hired, the plaintiff was able to perform, and did perform, the essential functions of her job.

7.   The plaintiff had a seizure on August 24, YR-2, while at work.

8.   On August 24, after the plaintiff's seizure, Leona Odell, the defendant's director, suspended the plaintiff without pay.

9.   On that same date, August 24, Leona Odell told the plaintiff that she could return to work if she provided a doctor's note stating that she would never have another seizure at work.

10.   On August 30, the plaintiff gave Leona Odell a note from her physician stating that she could safely perform the essential functions of the job.

11.   Upon reading this note, Leona Odell offered the plaintiff a demotion to the position of assistant teacher in the four year old classroom at a substantially reduced salary.

12.   The plaintiff reluctantly agreed to accept this demotion on August 31.

13.   That same day, August 31, the plaintiff sent a brief farewell letter to the parents of her two year olds.

14.   On September 2, YR-2, the day the plaintiff was scheduled to report to work in her new position, Leona Odell called her at home and fired her.

15.   Leona Odell's stated reason for firing the plaintiff was insubordination for sending the farewell letter.

16.   Leona Odell's stated reason for firing the plaintiff was a pretext for disability discrimination.

17.   As a result of the defendant's actions, the plaintiff has lost wages and fringe benefits and has suffered humiliation, embarrassment, and emotional pain and anguish.

Causes of Action

18.   The defendant discriminated against the plaintiff in violation of the Americans with Disabilities Act by demoting her and terminating her employment because of her disability.

19.   The plaintiff has exhausted her administrative remedies.

<u>Demand for Relief</u>

WHEREFORE, the plaintiff claims:

(a)   A declaratory judgment holding that the defendant's demotion and dismissal of Jean Jones is unlawful discrimination in violation of the ADA;

(b)   Reinstatement with full back pay and benefits;

(c)   Compensatory damages;

(d)   Reasonable attorneys' fees, including litigation expenses and costs;

(e)   Such other relief as the interests of justice require.

THE PLAINTIFF,
JEAN JONES

By: _____

Attorney for Plaintiff
Federal Bar No. NI 36963
93 Greyhound Way
Nita City, Nita 39396
(333) 666-9999

UNITED STATES DISTRICT COURT
DISTRICT OF NITA

JEAN JONES,   :   CIVIL NO. N-93-96369 (ABC)
     Plaintiff,   :

v.   :

KIDS-R-OURS, INC.,   :   OCTOBER 12, YR-2
     Defendant   :

ANSWER

1.   The defendant admits that the plaintiff has brought this action under Title I of the Americans with Disabilities Act. The defendant denies the remaining allegations of paragraph 1.

2.   The defendant admits the allegations of paragraph 2.

3.   The defendant admits the allegations of paragraph 3.

4.   The defendant admits the allegations of paragraph 4.

5.   The defendant admits the allegations of paragraph 5.

6.   The defendant denies the allegations of paragraph 6.

7.   The defendant admits the allegations of paragraph 7.

8.   The defendant admits the allegations of paragraph 8.

9.   The defendant denies the allegations of paragraph 9.

10.   The defendant admits that on August 30, YR-2, the plaintiff gave Leona Odell a note from her physician. The defendant denies the remaining allegations of paragraph 10.

11.   The defendant admits that Leona Odell offered the plaintiff a position as assistant teacher in the four year old classroom. The defendant denies the remaining allegations of paragraph 11.

12.   The defendant admits that the plaintiff accepted the new position on August 31, YR-2. The defendant lacks sufficient knowledge to admit or deny the remaining allegations of paragraph 12 and leaves the plaintiff to her proof.

13.   The defendant admits that the plaintiff sent a letter to parents on August 31, YR-2. The defendant denies the remaining allegations of paragraph 13.

14.   The defendant admits the allegations of paragraph 14.

15.   The defendant admits that the stated reason for firing the plaintiff was insubordination. The defendant denies the remaining allegations of paragraph 15.

16.   The defendant denies the allegations of paragraph 16.

17.   The defendant lacks sufficient knowledge to admit or deny the allegations of paragraph 17, and leaves the plaintiff to her proof.

18.   The defendant denies the allegations of paragraph 18.

19.   The defendant admits the allegations of paragraph 19.

AFFIRMATIVE DEFENSES

1.   Providing accommodation, other than the reassignment actually offered to and accepted by the plaintiff, would impose an undue hardship on the defendant's business operation.

2.   The plaintiff posed a direct threat to the health or safety of other individuals in the two year old classroom.

3.   The defendant would have discharged the plaintiff even if she did not have a disability.

THE DEFENDANT,
KIDS-R-OURS

By: *Susan O'Toole*

Attorney for Defendant
Federal Bar No. NI 96369
39 Corporate Place
Nita City, Nita 39396
(333) 999-6666

CERTIFICATION OF SERVICE

I hereby certify that a copy of the foregoing answer was mailed first class, postage prepaid, on this 12th day of October, YR-2, to Attorney for Plaintiff, 93 Greyhound Way, Nita City, Nita 39396.

Susan O'Toole

Attorney for Defendant

1   My name is Jean Jones. I reside with my parents, Harold and Carol Jones, at 100 Runner
2 Road, Nita City, Nita. I lived there until I went away to college and moved back in May of YR-
3 2. I am not married. The only other person who lives in the house is our dog, Grover.
4
5   I graduated in June of YR-5 from Nita City High School. The following September, I
6 began attending Lancaster College in Central City, about 100 miles north of Nita City. I was a
7 full-time student in their Early Childhood Education Program for two years. The program
8 included a classwork component as well as three separate field placements, or internships, at
9 local area child care centers. These internships are detailed on my resume. During the summer
10 of YR-4, I worked as a camp counselor. That is also on my resume. I never had a seizure at
11 work in any of these positions. I completed the Lancaster College program and received an
12 associate's degree in June of YR-3.
13
14   After graduation I took a summer job at the Oakwood Community School in Central City.
15 I worked there from June, YR-3, until the summer program ended in August. I did have one
16 seizure there. I don't remember anything about the seizure except that it happened while the
17 children were eating lunch. It didn't seem to be a problem for my employer, although someone
18 called an ambulance, which isn't necessary when I have a seizure.
19
20   My next job was at Bright Horizons Day Care Center, also in Central City. I worked
21 there from November, YR-3, through May, YR-2. I didn't have any seizures at Bright Horizons
22 and I think that my employer, Bobby Gerant, was quite pleased with my work there. The reason I
23 left was to move back to Nita City to be closer to my parents.
24
25   I have had a seizure disorder since I was six years old. I have complex partial seizure
26 disorder. It is largely controlled by medications. I take both Dilantin, 100 milligrams twice a
27 day, and Depakote, 250 milligrams four times each day. Still, I have three or four seizures a year.
28 The longest I have ever been seizure-free is nine months, when I was in college. I used to have
29 many more before I started taking Depakote when I was a teenager. About half of my seizures
30 are preceded by an aura. In my case, this is a kind of funny feeling in my stomach -- it's hard to
31 describe, but it's an unmistakable premonition that a seizure is coming in a few minutes.
32
33   I've been told that my seizures last two or three minutes. During that time I am in a
34 trance-like state, unaware of my surroundings but not unconscious. I do not fall down. I've been
35 told that I babble occasionally. In an emergency, I could be guided out of the room under my
36 own power. After two or three minutes I become aware of my surroundings but then need about
37 five more minutes to fully get my bearings. It's kind of like waking up in the morning. Then I
38 am fine. There are no after effects and I do not need medical treatment.
39

---

*This deposition transcript was excerpted so that only the deponent's answers are reprinted here. Assume this deposition was taken on March 14, YR-1, by defense counsel; that all applicable Federal Rules of Civil Procedure were followed; that this is a true and accurate rendering of the deponent's answers; and that the deponent read and signed this transcript.

1   The neurologist who treats my epilepsy is P.R. Gray, M.D. I have been seeing Dr. Gray
2 since I was eighteen years old. Before that I had a pediatric neurologist. Dr. Gray has told me
3 not to engage in dangerous activities, drive, or swim alone. Not being able to drive is really
4 inconvenient; I can't get to work or to the store unless someone gives me a ride. Dr. Gray has
5 also told me that it will be difficult for me to have children since it is not a good idea to take
6 epilepsy medications when you are pregnant.
7

8   In July of YR-2, after moving back home, I applied for a position at Kids-R-Ours Day
9 Care Center in Nita City. I sent my resume to Kids-R-Ours after reading an ad in the *Nita City*
10 *News*. I was interviewed by Leona Odell, director of the day care center. I am sure I told Leona
11 about my seizure condition. I must have, because I always give this information to prospective
12 employers to avoid any surprises. She told me generally about the job but did not show me any
13 written job description. I don't recall Leona saying anything about lifting children being a
14 requirement for the job. She didn't ask me if I had a driver's license.
15

16   I was hired to work as Head Teacher in Room 2, the two year old classroom. My salary
17 was $440 per week plus health insurance. I think my first day of work was July 19, YR-2. There
18 were sixteen children in Room 2, ranging in age from eighteen to thirty-six months. The room
19 was divided by movable partitions with one group of eight children on each side. All the adults
20 could easily see over the partitions. Each group was supervised at all times by at least two adults.
21

22   My normal work day began at 8:00 a.m. The children usually trickle in between 7:00 and
23 9:00. (Two assistant teachers in Room 2 started work at 7:00.) As the children come in, we help
24 them take off their coats and sweaters and hang them up in their cubby-holes. Then the children
25 are free to do different activities in various parts of the room such as blocks, dolls, trucks, dress-
26 up, art, etc. After a while we have circle time, where we might read a story or do a musical
27 activity, for example. The children get a snack of juice and cookies at 10:00. After that they go
28 back to activities. We eat lunch around noon. After clean-up, we pull out mats and the children
29 nap for about an hour. The afternoon is basically the same as the morning, with another snack
30 around 3:00 p.m. The children get to play outside in the yard at least once a day, usually for
31 around forty-five minutes, as long as weather permits. There is a door that opens directly into the
32 yard from Room 2; it is kept unlocked because it's a fire exit too.
33

34   I worked with an assistant teacher who did basically the same things that I did except I
35 was responsible for planning the activities and reporting to parents. In the classroom both of us
36 worked with the children in the same ways. To my understanding, the reason that there were two
37 of us in the room is that state regulations require that there is one adult present for every four
38 children in the eighteen to thirty-six month age group.
39

40   I can't think of too many situations where I would be left "alone" with the children. The
41 only times I can think of are when the assistant teacher has to take an older child to the bathroom.
42 Most of the kids are still in diapers, though, and we change them in the classroom. Another time
43 I might be alone with the children is if one child is sick and has to go to the office. Even then,
44 however, the teachers on the other side of the partition would probably be in the room.

1   Everything was going well with my job until August 24, when I had a seizure at work. It
2 happened sometime in the afternoon. It wasn't a big deal, and I continued working until the end
3 of the day. This seizure was pretty typical, like I described earlier.
4
5   After I got home on August 24, I received a call from Leona Odell. She said that she had
6 learned that I had had a seizure that day and was worried about the children. She asked me why I
7 had never told her about my condition. I said that I had mentioned it at the job interview. Leona
8 got very angry and started asking me a lot of questions about my seizure disorder, which I
9 answered truthfully. Leona then told me she was suspending me without pay until I brought her a
10 doctor's note stating that I would never have another seizure at work. She said there was no way
11 I could safely work with such young children in my condition.
12
13   I was really shocked and hurt. I couldn't believe that Leona had reacted so angrily and
14 unfairly. The next day I felt numb but nevertheless was able to call Dr. Gray to explain what had
15 happened. Dr. Gray said that Leona's action seemed outrageous and promised to write a note. I
16 received the note a couple of days later. The note did not say that I'd never have another seizure
17 at work, of course, but it made it clear that I could safely work with the children.
18
19   On Monday, August 30, I brought the note to Leona. Leona seemed much calmer than
20 she had been on the 24th. After reading the note, she reiterated her opinion that I could not work
21 with two year olds in my condition. Leona said she would try to find a position for me in Room
22 4 with the four to six year old children, but that it would be as an assistant teacher at a lower
23 hourly pay rate, $8.50 instead of $11, and would entail fewer hours per week (thirty instead of
24 forty). I told her I would think about it and get back to her in a couple of days.
25
26   That evening, I discussed the pros and cons of Leona's offer with my parents. I was pretty
27 upset. I thought that Leona was being unreasonable and unfair, and that there was no reason why
28 I couldn't continue working with the younger children. Not only do I prefer working with
29 toddlers, but the new job Leona had offered me represented a substantial cut in pay. It was also
30 humiliating to be told that I "couldn't safely work with these children." My parents, on the other
31 hand, encouraged me to take the job until I could find something else.
32
33   The next morning I called Leona and told her I would reluctantly accept her offer. She
34 said I should report to Room 4 on Thursday morning, September 2. I then wrote a farewell letter
35 to all the parents of my two year old class. I mailed the letters later that morning.
36
37   Late Wednesday afternoon, Leona called. She said that I had violated a company policy
38 by sending a letter directly to the parents. She said that she considered this to be insubordination
39 and that my employment was being terminated effective immediately. I protested that I had not
40 even considered the policy when I wrote the letter. I was too upset; I certainly didn't mean to be
41 insubordinate. Leona said she was sorry, but that her mind was made up. She said that the
42 policy is contained in the packet of materials that all new employees are given on their first day
43 of work and that it is posted outside her office.

1   After I got off the phone, I looked through all my papers relating to Kids-R-Ours and
2 could not find this policy. Although I was aware of the policy, I am sure that I never received a
3 copy of it. I don't know if it is posted on the bulletin board. I certainly had no idea that you
4 could be fired for violating this policy, especially unintentionally.
5
6   I still don't understand why Leona thought I couldn't safely care for the two year old
7 children. Dr. Gray only put two limitations on what I could do, lifting and carrying and staying
8 alone for more than a few minutes. As far as the latter is concerned, I was never alone with the
9 kids for more than a few minutes. As far as lifting and carrying, I had already worked out ways
10 of caring for the children without lifting them. For example, I would try to change diapers on a
11 mat on the floor. If a child needed a hug, I would sit on the floor to hug her.
12
13   I've been unable to find work since Leona fired me. At first I was too traumatized to even
14 look for another job. I made a new year's resolution, however, at my therapist's suggestion, to get
15 out there and pound the pavement, and since January I've been diligently doing so without
16 success. I didn't collect any unemployment compensation because I hadn't worked at Kids-R-
17 Ours long enough. Basically, my parents have been supporting me and paying my medical bills,
18 which would have been covered under the insurance I lost when Leona fired me. I wasn't able to
19 afford to continue my health insurance under COBRA.
20
21   Being without medical insurance is very stressful for me since I take so much medication
22 for epilepsy. This is on top of the feelings I've had of anger, hopelessness and humiliation over
23 the way Leona treated me. I've had difficulty sleeping, loss of appetite, frequent crying episodes,
24 and strained relationships with my family and friends. My therapist, Dr. Henry, has been helping
25 me with all this but progress has been slow. I'm determined to move on and become independent
26 again.

     This deposition was taken in the office of plaintiff's counsel under oath on March 14,
YR-1.

     I have read the foregoing transcript of my deposition given on the date above and find it is
a true and accurate representation of my testimony.

     Signed this _____ day of _____ YR-___ at Nita City, Nita.

_____
JEAN JONES, Deponent

Certified by:

_____
ROGER DAVIS
Certified Shorthand Reporter, (CSR)

DEPOSITION OF LEONA ODELL[*]

1   My name is Leona Odell. I am the Director of Kids-R-Ours, Inc., a day care center
2 located at 100 Center Street in Nita City, Nita. Kids-R-Ours is a nonprofit corporation run by a
3 board of directors. The board's main functions are to establish policy, approve budgets, and hire
4 and fire the director. I am solely responsible for the day-to-day management of the corporation,
5 including all personnel decisions such as hiring and firing. I have been Director since Kids-R-
6 Ours' inception in YR-11.
7
8   The Kids-R-Ours board has approved policies on a variety of subjects. I can think of
9 only two that bear directly or indirectly on this case. One policy prohibits all forms of illegal
10 discrimination. That policy was approved by the board two or three years ago. Another policy,
11 approved many years ago, prohibits employees from sending announcements, bulletins, or
12 newsletters to parents without prior approval of the director. The purpose of that policy, which is
13 titled "Written Communications," is to provide some centralized oversight of official
14 communications sent out by the day care center. I routinely give copies of these policies to new
15 employees. Also, these two policies and several others are posted on the bulletin board in the
16 corridor outside my office.
17
18   Kids-R-Ours' annual budget currently approaches $1,000,000. In YR-2, when Jean Jones
19 was employed at Kids-R-Ours, I believe our income was about $800,000. All our income comes
20 from payments made by families of our children. Our biggest expenditure is, of course,
21 personnel costs.
22
23   The day care center is a one-story, free-standing building located in a quiet, mostly
24 residential area of Nita City. There are four classrooms, an entry-way, and a small office.
25 Rooms 1 and 2 share a bathroom, as do Rooms 3 and 4. A staff bathroom is located just outside
26 the office. Each classroom has two exits, one to the interior and one to the play yard outside.
27 The yard is surrounded by a chain-link fence to protect the children from running out into the
28 street.
29
30   There are two groups of children in each classroom. Classrooms are divided roughly in
31 half by movable partitions four foot high, and each group stays primarily on one side of the
32 partition. State regulations control teacher-student ratios. In Room 1, which has children aged
33 six weeks to eighteen months -- we call it the infant room -- the maximum ratio is 1:4. The same
34 ratio applies in Room 2, the quote two year old classroom, which has children aged eighteen to
35 thirty-six months. In Room 3, the three year old room, with children aged thirty-six to forty-eight
36 months, the maximum ratio is 1:8. The same ratio applies in Room 4, the four year old
37 classroom, where the children range from forty-eight to seventy-two months. Because of these
38 state-mandated ratios and the limited number of rooms in our building, Kids-R-Ours can only
39 care for a certain number of children, and there is always a waiting list to get in.

---

[*]This deposition transcript was excerpted so that only the deponent's answers are reprinted here. Assume
that this deposition was taken on March 14, YR-1, by plaintiff's counsel; that all applicable Federal Rules of Civil
Procedure were followed; that this is a true and accurate rendering of the deponent's answers; and that the deponent
read and signed this transcript.

1   Two head teachers and four assistant teachers are assigned to each classroom. However,
2   they don't all work the same hours. Basically, I set up the schedule so that two assistants arrive at
3   7:00 a.m., after which the first children begin to arrive, and leave at noon. The two head teachers
4   arrive at 8:00 a.m. and work until 5:00 p.m. Two different assistants arrive at noon and work
5   until 6:00 p.m., by which time the last children have left. This way, there are always enough staff
6   in each classroom to satisfy the state ratios. The day care center has a full-time assistant director,
7   who, like me, works from 8:30 a.m. to 5:30 p.m. There is also a custodian working in the
8   building from noon to 5 p.m.
9

10   At the end of June, YR-2, one of the head teachers in the two year old classroom resigned
11   effective July 16. After I received her resignation, I placed an ad in the *Nita Times* seeking
12   another head teacher. I received about fifteen or so resumes and interviewed three women for the
13   job. Jean Jones was the third woman I interviewed. I don't remember too many specific details
14   about the interview, but I do remember that Jean said nothing about having epilepsy. I also know
15   I gave her a copy of the written job description because I always give that to prospective
16   employees. I know I was impressed enough by her educational background, experience and
17   personal qualities to contact a couple of the references she provided me. Bobby Gerant, the one
18   that I was able to reach, raved about her so I offered Jean the position. She started work on
19   Monday, July 19.
20

21   On August 24, J. Shoney, one of Jean's assistant teachers, came into my office in the late
22   afternoon. I knew something was up because she closed the door behind her. She seemed very
23   upset. Shoney told me that she thought Jean had suffered a seizure earlier that afternoon during
24   the middle of class. She said that Jean had been non-responsive, glassy-eyed and mumbling
25   incoherently for several minutes. I think Shoney said it lasted four or five minutes. After that it
26   took Jean several more minutes to collect herself and join the children and Shoney in a game.
27   Shoney said she was really thankful that Jean had told her about her seizure condition ahead of
28   time, or else she (Shoney) would not have known what was happening.
29

30   I asked Shoney what she knew about Jean's seizure condition and a few other questions. I
31   do remember that my reaction was one of surprise, since Jean had never told <u>me</u> about any
32   seizure condition. I was very concerned, obviously, about the safety and welfare of the children.
33   I'm not sure I would have hired Jean if I'd known she had a seizure condition. At a minimum, I
34   would have wanted to know a lot more about the nature, frequency, and severity of her seizures.
35

36   After Shoney left my office, I immediately called Jean. I told Jean that I had heard about
37   her seizure incident and was worried about the children. I asked her why she had never disclosed
38   to me that she had a seizure condition. Jean claimed that she had told me about it at her job
39   interview and generally downplayed the significance of the whole thing. I did get very angry.
40   There is no way that Jean had ever told me this; this is certainly something I would have
41   remembered. In response to my questions, Jean said that she had had the condition since early
42   childhood. She said that she had about two seizures a year, and that the seizures were not severe.
43   When I asked her what "not severe" meant, Jean said that the seizures were short in duration and
44   that she didn't fall down.

1   Based on this, I told Jean that I did not believe she could safely supervise two year old
2   children. I told her I had no choice but to suspend her. I said that I would allow Jean to return to
3   work if she could provide a note from her physician stating that it was safe for Jean to work with
4   two year olds. I do not recall asking for a guarantee that Jean would never have another seizure
5   at work.
6
7   On Monday, August 30, Jean came in with a note from her neurologist. I don't remember
8   now exactly what the note said, but it certainly did not say that Jean could safely work with two
9   year olds. I think it may have said that any danger posed by Jean could be eliminated if she didn't
10 lift or carry children, and if she was never left alone with them.
11
12   I considered this unacceptable and told Jean so. Lifting and carrying children are
13 absolutely essential functions of working with two year olds. You can see by the job description
14 that we expect head teachers to be able to lift and carry children. I told Jean that under no
15 circumstances would I permit her to work with two year olds.
16
17   I felt bad for Jean, however, and wanted to make some kind of accommodation. It so
18 happened that one of the afternoon assistant teachers in the four year old classroom had just
19 resigned and I needed to fill the position. I offered Jean this position. I felt that Jean could work
20 safely with children aged four years and up since they generally don't need to be lifted and
21 carried. Also, children that age generally don't require the same kind of intensive supervision as
22 their younger counterparts. Jean wanted to know how much this position paid, and I told her. I
23 think it was around $8.50 per hour at the time. Jean said she would have to think about it. The
24 next day she called and said she would accept. We agreed that she would return to work in her
25 new position on Thursday morning, September 2.
26
27   I did consider several other possible accommodations for Jean, including switching her
28 and one of the head teachers in the four year old classroom. I went so far as to discuss this
29 possibility with each of those head teachers. Both of them felt that it would be inappropriate to
30 make this switch for a number of reasons. For one thing, both of them were very experienced
31 working with that particular age group and strongly preferred it. Also, it would have been unfair
32 to the children. Finally, although the job of head teacher has a generic job description for all
33 levels, the jobs are really quite different. It would have been like switching a sixth grade
34 elementary school teacher with a third grade teacher.
35
36   On Wednesday, September 1, I received a call from Joyce Staples, the parent of a child in
37 the four year old class. She was very upset. Apparently Jean had written a letter to the parents of
38 the two year old class and Joyce Staples had gotten a copy of it from a friend. Joyce read the
39 letter to me over the phone. The letter said that I had reassigned Jean to the four year old
40 classroom because of her seizure condition and that Jean was not happy with that decision. Joyce
41 was upset because she did not believe her daughter would be safe in Jean's care. She made it
42 very plain that she would pull her daughter out of the day care center if Jean went to work in the
43 four year old classroom. She said she had spoken to two other parents who shared her concern.

1   I tried to calm Joyce down a bit. I explained to her that she did not have all the facts. I
2 told her that Jean probably would <u>not</u> be going to work in the four year old class and that I would
3 call her back later in the day. I wanted to see the letter itself before making any final decision,
4 and Joyce was kind enough to offer to bring me in her copy. I did not tell Joyce <u>why</u> Jean would
5 not be coming back to work; I saw no reason to do this, and frankly it seemed like better
6 customer relations to leave Joyce with the impression that Jean had never been offered a job in
7 the four year old class in the first place.
8
9   In fact, the reason why I had tentatively decided that Jean would not be coming back to
10 work was that her letter was grossly insubordinate. In addition, it violated the company policy
11 regarding written communications to parents.
12
13   Later that morning, Wednesday, Joyce Staples brought the letter to my office. Seeing the
14 letter confirmed my suspicion that I would have to fire Jean. I then called Jean at home and told
15 her that her employment was terminated.
16
17   I never have had occasion to discipline any other employee for violating the policy on
18 written communications. I have, however, involuntarily terminated two other employees over the
19 years. One of them, Garrett Griswold, was a janitor who worked at Kids-R-Ours for about six
20 months and whose job performance was unsatisfactory. The other, whose name I can't remember
21 at the moment, was an assistant teacher who had a problem with tardiness. This employee failed
22 to correct the problem despite my repeated warnings and had to be terminated.
23
24   I received a B.A. in early childhood education from the University of Nita in YR-17. I
25 worked in various day care jobs between then and YR-11. I have two daughters aged ten and
26 twelve.
27
28   We have separate job descriptions for the positions of head teacher and assistant teacher.
29 The job descriptions are very similar, the main difference being that head teachers have
30 responsibility for planning and everything that goes on in the classroom. They also are
31 responsible for communicating with parents about individual children. Other than that, the jobs
32 are basically the same. If you went into a classroom, you probably wouldn't be able to tell who
33 was the head teacher and who was the assistant teacher.
34
35   The job descriptions are generic. What I mean by this is that they're not specific by age or
36 classroom. Of course, what a teacher would actually have to do in the infant room is very
37 different from what she would have to do in the four year old classroom. Obviously, there would
38 be more lifting and carrying with the younger children, which is part of the reason why I thought
39 that Jean Jones could safely work with four year olds but not two year olds. Also, there are more
40 situations where the teacher might have to go out of the room with a child -- for instance, to take
41 him to the bathroom -- in the two year old classroom.

1   I am somewhat familiar with the Americans with Disabilities Act and the obligations it
2   places on employers. I know that employers have to make reasonable accommodations for
3   handicapped people. I did consider several other accommodations for Jean other than
4   reassigning her to the four year old class but I couldn't think of any that would work besides
5   hiring additional staff. With an agency our size, unfortunately, that is not possible.

        This deposition was taken in the office of plaintiff's counsel under oath on March 14,
YR-1.

        I have read the foregoing transcript of my deposition given on the date above and find it is
a true and accurate representation of my testimony.

        Signed this _____ day of _____ YR-____ at Nita City, Nita.

                        _Leona Odell_____
                        LEONA ODELL, Deponent

                        Certified by:

                        _Roger Davis_____
                        ROGER DAVIS
                        Certified Shorthand Reporter, (CSR)

DEPOSITION OF P.R. GRAY, M.D.[*]

1   My name is P.R. Gray. I am a physician specializing in neurology, and am board-
2 certified in neurology and psychiatry. I practice with several other neurologists in a group called
3 the Nita Neurological Group, Inc., with offices in Nita City, Nita.
4
5   I have been treating Jean Jones for approximately the last five years. Jean has partial
6 complex seizure disorder that results in psychomotor attacks, which are less severe than grand
7 mal seizures. Psychomotor attacks are focal seizures characterized by a one or two minute loss
8 of contact with surroundings. The patient is mentally confused, may stagger, perform
9 purposeless movements, and make unintelligible sounds. The patient will not understand what is
10 said and may refuse aid. These attacks can develop at any age and are associated with structural
11 lesions in the temporal lobe.
12
13   Some patients experience an aura between a few seconds and several hours prior to a
14 seizure. An aura is a subjective sensation such as a peculiar smell, vision, taste, or feeling that
15 precedes a seizure.
16
17   In Jean's case, she has two or three seizures a year. During the seizures, she becomes
18 unaware of her surroundings but doesn't fall to the ground as happens in grand mal seizures. She
19 may also mumble. Jean and her parents also report that Jean is somewhat dazed when she comes
20 out of a seizure, and that it may take as long as four or five minutes for her to be ready to resume
21 normal activity. Jean describes this period as similar to waking up in the morning. This is not at
22 all uncommon for patients with partial complex seizure disorder. Prior to a seizure, Jean
23 sometimes experiences a distinctive feeling in her stomach that tells her a seizure is about to
24 occur.
25
26   Jean's current treatment consists of two medications, Dilantin and Depakote. She is
27 prescribed 100 milligrams of Dilantin twice a day, and 250 milligrams of Depakote four times a
28 day. This medication regimen has reduced the number of Jean's seizures but has not eliminated
29 them. Occasionally Jean still has more frequent seizures.
30
31   Over the years, I have treated hundreds if not thousands of adult patients with one form or
32 another of epilepsy. Most of these patients have been able to live seizure-free with appropriate
33 medication. Among those patients who still have seizures, some have been able to work in
34 highly demanding jobs, while others have been unable to work at all. Much depends upon the
35 frequency and severity of the particular patient's seizures.

---

[*]This deposition transcript was excerpted so that only the deponent's answers are reprinted here. Assume that this deposition was taken on March 14, YR-1, by defense counsel; that all applicable Federal Rules of Civil Procedure were followed; that this is a true and accurate rendering of the deponent's answers; and that the deponent read and signed this transcript. **Further assume that Dr. Gray died on September 12, YR-1.**

1   I am obviously not an expert on day care centers. However, I have seen day care centers
2   in operation with my own children. I have never been to Kids-R-Ours. Given the relative
3   infrequency of Jean Jones' seizures and their relative lack of severity, I don't believe that her
4   seizures posed any real risk to the children. After all, anyone can become suddenly ill or
5   distracted. Furthermore, any theoretical risk that Jean's seizures posed to the children could have
6   been eliminated by having her not lift the children and not remain alone with them for more than
7   a few minutes at a time. I certainly would feel comfortable leaving my own kids at a day care
8   center where Jean worked.

This deposition was taken in the office of plaintiff's counsel under oath on March 14, YR-1.

I have read the foregoing transcript of my deposition given on the date above and find it is a true and accurate representation of my testimony.

Signed this _____ day of _____ YR-___ at Nita City, Nita.

_____
P.R. GRAY, Deponent

Certified by:

_____
ROGER DAVIS
Certified Shorthand Reporter, (CSR)

DEPOSITION OF JOYCE STAPLES[*]

1   My name is Joyce Staples. My husband Frank and I are the parents of Cameron Staples,
2 age four, and Casey Staples, age six months. I work as a store manager for Store 24, a twenty-
3 four hour convenience store. Cameron and Casey both attend day care at Kids-R-Ours. Casey
4 started when she was six weeks old.
5
6   In August of YR-2, I received a phone call from my friend Mary Stovell, whose child was
7 in the two year old class at Kids-R-Ours. I can't remember the exact date, but I know I was off
8 work that day. Mary was upset about a letter she had just received from Jean Jones, her
9 daughter's head teacher. The letter said that Leona Odell, the director of Kids-R-Ours, had
10 demoted Jean to the position of assistant teacher in the four year old class because Jean had had
11 an epileptic seizure at work. Although Mary thought that Jean was a good teacher, she had not
12 known that Jean was an epileptic and was very upset that Leona would have made someone with
13 such a handicap responsible for small children. She thought that I might want to know that Jean
14 would now be working in Cameron's class. I asked Mary to drop off a copy of the letter, which
15 she did within a few minutes.
16
17   After I received the letter, I called the mothers of two other children in Cameron's class.
18 They were also shocked to learn that somebody with epileptic seizures would be caring for their
19 children. We agreed that I would call Leona Odell and express our concerns.
20
21   I then called Leona Odell. I told her about Jean's letter, which she didn't seem to know
22 about. I explained that I did not understand how an epileptic could work with young children. I
23 told her there was no way I would allow my child to be exposed to such a risk, and that I and
24 others would definitely remove our children from the day care center if Jean were not fired.
25
26   Leona seemed surprisingly calm under the circumstances. She mostly asked me a lot of
27 questions; I don't remember most of them now. I know she asked me whom I'd spoken to about
28 this, and how many other parents knew about Jean's letter. By the end of the conversation, I had
29 the impression that Leona was going to fire Jean in response to the concerns of the parents. I
30 distinctly remember Leona saying that Jean probably would not be going to work in the four year
31 old class. Leona said she wanted to see a copy of the letter before making any final decision, and
32 I agreed to drop it off with her, which I did later that day.
33
34   I did not know, until you just told me, that the official reason that Leona fired Jean was
35 insubordination for writing the letter. I don't believe that was the real reason that Jean was fired,
36 however. I think the real reason was that Leona was scared that a lot of parents would pull their
37 kids out of the day care center if Jean remained employed there. I do feel sorry for Jean -- I think
38 she's a nice person and all -- but the safety of the children has to come first.

---

[*]This deposition transcript was excerpted so that only the deponent's answers are reprinted here. Assume
this deposition was taken on March 14, YR-1, by plaintiff's counsel; that all applicable Federal Rules of Civil
Procedure were followed; that this is a true and accurate rendering of the deponent's answers; and that the deponent
read and signed this transcript.

1   I was convicted of a crime in YR-9. I was in college at the time, and my boyfriend was a
2 cocaine user. I started using drugs to be part of his crowd. The police busted a party we were
3 attending, and I was arrested for possession of cocaine. After successfully completing a
4 rehabilitation program, I pled guilty and was sentenced to two years' probation. I still attend NA
5 meetings and, although I still consider myself a recovering addict, I haven't used any drugs at all
6 ever since.

This deposition was taken in the office of plaintiff's counsel under oath on March 14, YR-1.

I have read the foregoing transcript of my deposition given on the date above and find it is a true and accurate representation of my testimony.

Signed this _____ day of _____ YR-___ at Nita City, Nita.

_____
JOYCE STAPLES, Deponent

Certified by:

_____
ROGER DAVIS
Certified Shorthand Reporter, (CSR)

DEPOSITION OF KIM GREEN[*]

1   My name is Kim Green. I am Director of the Summer Program at the Oakwood
2 Community School in Central City, Nita. Oakwood is a public school that runs enrichment
3 programs for children during the summer. I have been Director of the Summer Program there
4 since YR-9. I teach a third-grade class during the school year.
5
6   Jean Jones worked under my supervision in the summer program from June, YR-3, to
7 August, YR-3. She was a counselor working with a group of four and five year olds. Her
8 responsibilities consisted of planning and supervising the children's indoor and outdoor activities,
9 including field trips.
10
11   When I hired Jean Jones, she did not tell me that she had epilepsy. I remember this
12 because I was very surprised and shocked when she had a seizure at work one day. Also, I
13 always ask new hires whether or not they have any disabilities that may interfere with their work
14 or the children's safety.
15
16   Jean's work with the children was generally good. She seemed to have a nice way with
17 the kids, although she did let things get a bit wild at times.
18
19   Late in August -- it was the very last day of the summer program, in fact -- Jean had a
20 seizure. I personally witnessed this. It was during a kickball game. Jean was pitching; I was
21 half-watching from about twenty-five yards away. All of a sudden I noticed that the game had
22 stopped. Jean was just standing there, with the big red rubber kickball in her hands, not moving.
23 I started walking over toward her and noticed she was mumbling incoherently. Then she dropped
24 the ball. Jean looked blank, almost like she was hypnotized. I asked her several times if
25 something was the matter. When she didn't respond, I sent one of the kids inside to tell my
26 assistant to call 911.
27
28   After what seemed like an eternity, Jean seemed to snap to. I guided her over to a bench
29 where she sat down. Although groggy and seemingly stunned, Jean explained to me that she had
30 had an epileptic seizure and that it was nothing to worry about. When the ambulance came a few
31 minutes later, Jean refused treatment.
32
33   I don't know how long exactly this whole episode lasted. The seizure obviously was
34 already in progress by the time I noticed that the game had stopped. Given that, I would assume
35 that the seizure itself lasted a good five minutes. The kids were very upset by the whole episode.
36 They didn't know what was going on.

---

[*]This deposition transcript was excerpted so that only the deponent's answers are reprinted here. Assume this deposition was taken on March 14, YR-1, by defense counsel; that all applicable Federal Rules of Civil Procedure were followed; that this is a true and accurate rendering of the deponent's answers; and that the deponent read and signed this transcript.

1   Fortunately this happened on the last day of the summer. I say fortunately because I
2 definitely would have had to fire Jean had it not been the last day anyway. I personally don't see
3 how you can have an epileptic working anywhere near children. To me that would be like having
4 a blind bus driver.

        This deposition was taken in the office of plaintiff's counsel under oath on March 14,
YR-1.

        I have read the foregoing transcript of my deposition given on the date above and find it is
a true and accurate representation of my testimony.

        Signed this _____ day of _____ YR-___ at Nita City, Nita.

_____
KIM GREEN, Deponent

Certified by:

_____
ROGER DAVIS
Certified Shorthand Reporter, (CSR)

DEPOSITION OF E. HEMINGWAY[*]

1   My name is E. Hemingway. I currently work at Kinderplotz, a day care center in Nita
2 City, Nita. I am a head teacher with three year olds. Previously, I was a head teacher at Kids-R-
3 Ours, Inc., for seven years. I resigned from Kids-R-Ours effective July 30, YR-2.
4

5   At both Kinderplotz and Kids-R-Ours, a head teacher supervises one or more assistant
6 teachers. A head teacher is also responsible for planning and implementing the children's
7 activities and reporting to parents.
8

9   At Kids-R-Ours, I worked in Classroom #2 with two year olds. I understand that Jean
10 Jones took my place in that classroom.
11

12   I seldom lifted children in the two year old class. In fact, I consciously avoided lifting
13 them because I have a bad back. A couple of times I have pulled a muscle in my back; my doctor
14 has told me to avoid straining it. This was never a problem at Kids-R-Ours. When a kid had to
15 be lifted for any reason, I would often ask the assistant teacher to do it, or I would just try to
16 improvise so I wouldn't have to lift. For example, if I wanted to hug a youngster, I would often
17 sit or kneel down on the floor. I never discussed this with Leona Odell because it didn't seem
18 necessary to do so. I was fully capable of performing my job. In an emergency, I could certainly
19 lift a child.
20

21   I've never before seen the job description for head teacher that you're now showing me. I
22 think the lifting requirements listed under "Physical Demands" are a joke. I never had a child in
23 the two year old class who weighed fifty pounds! I did occasionally lift lighter children, as I've
24 already stated. However, there was almost always somebody else nearby who could do the lifting
25 if it was necessary.
26

27   There were four adults assigned to Classroom #2 from 8:00 a.m. to 5:00 p.m. It would
28 have been rare that an adult would have been entirely alone with the children. For example, even
29 if my assistant teacher was out of the room, there would have been one or two teachers in the
30 other part of the room. The room was separated roughly in half by a movable partition
31 approximately five feet high. One could always call over to the other side of the room for
32 assistance.
33

34   I left Kids-R-Ours for a variety of reasons. My current job is higher paying and closer to
35 my home. Also, over the course of seven years I really had grown tired of working for Leona
36 Odell. I don't think Leona is a bad person, deep down, but she is a compulsive neatnick, a
37 busybody, and has absolutely no interpersonal skills. She's a real pain in the neck to work for. I
38 thought I kept the room fairly neat, but Leona was always complaining that things were out of
39 place and this and that. Also, Leona liked to have a lot of art on the walls because it impressed

---

[*]This deposition transcript was excerpted so that only the deponent's answers are reprinted here. Assume
this deposition was taken on March 14, YR-1, by defense counsel; that all applicable Federal Rules of Civil
Procedure were followed; that this is a true and accurate rendering of the deponent's answers; and that the deponent
read and signed this transcript.

1   the parents. When I left, Leona joked, "I hope I can train the next head teacher better than I
2   trained you." Can you believe it? The woman didn't even have the decency or grace to say a few
3   kind words after all the time I had worked there.
4
5   I don't know anything about why Garrett Griswold was terminated. He was a nice fellow
6   and seemed to keep the place clean. I understand he brought some kind of complaint against
7   Leona, but I don't really know anything about it.
8
9   I do know that Kids-R-Ours has a policy about written communications from staff
10   members to parents. My understanding of the policy is as follows: Teachers can send home
11   handwritten notes about individual children without approval. In fact, we were encouraged to do
12   so. More formal communications, like announcements, had to be cleared with Leona. I never
13   understood the policy to require that every communication sent to all parents had to be cleared.
14   For example, I and other head teachers usually sent holiday greetings to parents of children in our
15   classes. Leona knew of this practice and never said anything about it.
16
17   I do remember one teacher who sent home an announcement about some class activity
18   without getting Leona's approval. I think it was about a field trip. This was four or five years
19   ago. In any event, Leona got upset about this and circulated copies of the written policy. Yes,
20   the document you're now showing me is the policy I'm talking about. I was aware of the policy
21   before Leona circulated it. I'm not sure if it's posted on the bulletin board outside her office. It is
22   possible that the policy was given to me around the time I started working at Kids-R-Ours.
23
24   I've never seen the letter you're now showing me from Jean Jones to the parents. To be
25   perfectly honest, it does seem to be inappropriate at first glance. I can't tell you whether it
26   violates the policy or not, but I can certainly understand why Leona thought it was insubordinate.
27   Even so, it sounds like Leona overreacted by firing Jean. That's so typical of Leona!

        This deposition was taken in the office of plaintiff's counsel under oath on March 14,
YR-1.

        I have read the foregoing transcript of my deposition given on the date above and find it is
a true and accurate representation of my testimony.

        Signed this _____ day of _____ YR-___ at Nita City, Nita.

_E. Hemingway_____
E. HEMINGWAY, Deponent

Certified by:

_Roger Davis_____
ROGER DAVIS
Certified Shorthand Reporter, (CSR)

DEPOSITION OF J. SHONEY[*]

1   My name is J. Shoney. I am an assistant teacher at Kids-R-Ours, Inc., day care center, in
2 the two year old class. I have been working at Kids-R-Ours since January, YR-2. This is the
3 first full-time job I have had since I graduated from Nita City High School in June of YR-3.
4
5   An assistant teacher assists the head teachers in supervising and caring for the children.
6 The main difference between the two jobs is that the head teachers are responsible for planning
7 and reporting to parents.
8
9   During the summer of YR-2 I worked under the supervision of Jean Jones. I don't
10 remember the exact dates Jean was there, but it wasn't very long. Before that, E. Hemingway
11 was my supervisor. She left Kids for a better-paying day care job. Hemingway and Leona Odell
12 didn't get along too well; I don't really know why.
13
14   Jean and I were responsible for a group of approximately eight children in Classroom #2.
15 I worked from 12:00 to 6:00 p.m. I really liked Jean and don't want to say anything bad about
16 her. Jean was very good with the kids, and they responded well to her. As far as being a
17 supervisor, Jean was excellent. She really let me do my own thing and gave me a lot of
18 autonomy with the children.
19
20   Early on, I remember Jean telling me that she had some kind of seizures. I didn't really
21 make anything of this at the time; it only became significant in light of what happened later. I
22 think Jean told me that she occasionally had seizures but that they mostly happened at home and
23 that they weren't the really bad kind. You know, the kind where the person falls down and flops
24 all around and possibly bites their tongue and all. I can't remember why Jean told me this. Oh
25 yeah, it came up when I asked Jean why her parents picked her up from work all the time. She
26 said she couldn't get a driver's license, etc., and one thing led to another.
27
28   On what turned out to be Jean's last day of work, she had a seizure right in the middle of
29 class. The two of us were in the classroom with the eight children. Jean was sitting at a table in
30 the northeast area of the room, not far from the door to the bathroom, reading to some children. I
31 was playing with some children in the block corner. At first, I didn't realize what was going on.
32 Then I noticed that all the kids had become quiet and were staring at Jean. She had a glassy look
33 in her eyes and appeared to be mumbling something. I asked her if everything was okay, and she
34 didn't respond. That's when I realized she must be having a seizure.
35
36   I gathered the children up and moved them to another part of the room to play a game.
37 My main thought at the time was to distract their attention from Jean. I kept one eye on Jean to
38 make sure she was okay. She just kept sitting there with that blank look and mumbling
39 incoherently. It was hard to keep the children's attention. They kept wanting to know what was

---

[*]This deposition transcript was excerpted so that only the deponent's answers are reprinted here. Assume
that this deposition was taken on March 14, YR-1, by plaintiff's counsel; that all applicable Federal Rules of Civil
Procedure were followed; that this is a true and accurate rendering of the deponent's answers; and that the deponent
read and signed this transcript.

1 wrong with Jean. After several minutes -- three or four, I would guess -- Jean seemed to snap out
2 of it. I asked her again if she was okay, and this time she said yes, not to worry. She sat at the
3 table for a few more minutes and then joined me and the children in a game.
4
5 Later that day, after Jean had gone home, I did tell Leona what had happened. I did this
6 because of something that happened with Nina Johnson, the mother of one of our girls. When
7 Nina came to pick her daughter up late that afternoon, her daughter said to her, "There was
8 something wrong with Jean today." Nina asked me what the problem was, and I basically told a
9 white lie. I said that Jean hadn't felt well. Afterwards, I got nervous and decided that I'd better
10 say something to Leona.
11
12 I went into Leona's office and told her what had happened with Jean and Ms. Johnson.
13 Leona listened intently to what I said and asked me a lot of questions about what had happened.
14 She told me that if anyone else asked me about what had happened to Jean, to refer the person to
15 her. She also said not to say anything about our conversation to Jean. The whole conversation
16 didn't last more than five minutes. At the end, Leona thanked me and told me I had done the
17 right thing by coming to her.
18
19 The next day, Leona told all the staff that Jean had a medical problem and would be out
20 of work until it was resolved. I felt bad -- I mean, I hadn't wanted to get Jean in trouble or
21 anything. A substitute named Barbara Elliott came in for Jean that day.
22
23 The following week, I don't remember exactly which day, Leona told me that she had
24 been forced to terminate Jean and that Ms. Elliott would be the head teacher. Leona said it
25 would be inappropriate to discuss her reasons with me, but she assured me it had nothing to do
26 with Jean's seizure or anything that I had done. Leona told me to continue to refer parents to her
27 if they had questions.
28
29 I do think that lifting is an important part of a day care job, especially when you're caring
30 for two year olds. There are lots of situations where you have to lift kids: when you're changing
31 their diapers, when they need a hug, if they get hurt, etc. I don't really remember anything about
32 E. Hemingway having a bad back. We both lifted the children. It would be possible for one of
33 the teachers to do most, if not all, of the lifting. Of course, this wouldn't work if one of the
34 teachers was out of the room, which does happen.
35
36 I know that Kids-R-Ours has a policy about written communications to parents. It didn't
37 really affect me though since the head teachers were responsible for writing to parents. Leona
38 showed me the policy when I started working there. I don't know whether or not it's posted
39 outside Leona's office.
40
41 Actually, I've never seen the letter from Jean that you're showing me until now, although
42 I'd heard about it. I don't know whether it is a good enough reason to fire Jean. I take that back; I
43 don't really think I should get into that. I really love my job and do not want to lose it. I did talk
44 to Leona yesterday about this deposition. All she told me was to tell the truth and not to
45 volunteer any information.

This deposition was taken in the office of plaintiff's counsel under oath on March 14, YR-1.

I have read the foregoing transcript of my deposition given on the date above and find it is a true and accurate representation of my testimony.

Signed this _____ day of _____ YR-___ at Nita City, Nita.

_____
J. SHONEY, Deponent

Certified by:

_____
ROGER DAVIS
Certified Shorthand Reporter, (CSR)

KIDS-R-OURS, INC.

Job Description: Head Teacher

I.   Function

Plans and implements activities designed to promote social, physical, and intellectual growth of the children under his/her care. Responsible for the personal care, hygiene, learning and development activities, specialized programs, and discipline of the children. Maintains classroom records, cleanliness, and orderliness. Child care has special demands in that we care for children who cannot care for themselves. It is critical that all employees holding classroom teaching positions be mentally and physically fit to perform the duties outlined in this job description.

II.   Education/Experience Requirements

A. Is at least 20 years old (21 years old if responsible for driving a van).
B. Holds a high school diploma or the equivalent and is appropriately qualified for the assigned group through education, training, experience, and/or personal qualities.
C. Maintains state in-service requirements.

III. Physical Demands

A. Required to stand 75% of the work day.
B. Must occasionally lift or move children weighing up to 50 pounds, sometimes in awkward positions.
C. May occasionally be required to lift children weighing up to 60 pounds in emergency conditions.
D. Must be able to exercise with children on the playground and in the classroom.
E. Must be able physically and mentally to react immediately to unexpected and emergency circumstances.
F. Must be able to stoop and bend to a young child's level.

IV.   Job Requirements

A. Must support and implement the Kids-R-Ours educational philosophy.
B. Is responsible for providing a positive, loving, and nurturing environment for children.
C. Must display respect for children and adults.
D. Is responsible for maintaining classroom environment in a neat and inviting manner.
E. Is responsible for maintaining order and discipline in the classroom.
F. Must follow prescribed administrative procedures.
G. Must follow cleanliness procedures.

Adopted January, YR-6

KIDS-R-OURS, INC.

Job Description: Assistant Teacher

I.   Function

Implements activities designed to promote social, physical, and intellectual growth of the children under his/her care. Assists in the personal care, hygiene, learning and development activities, specialized programs, and discipline of the children. Helps maintain classroom cleanliness and orderliness. Child care has special demands in that we care for children who cannot care for themselves. It is critical that all employees holding classroom teaching positions be mentally and physically fit to perform the duties outlined in this job description.

II.   Education/Experience Requirements

A. Is at least 18 years old.

B. Is appropriately qualified for the assigned group through education, training, experience, and/or personal qualities.

C. Maintains state in-service requirements.

III.   Physical Demands

A. Required to stand 75% of the work day.

B. Must occasionally lift or move children weighing up to 50 pounds, sometimes in awkward positions.

C. May occasionally be required to lift children weighing up to 60 pounds in emergency conditions.

D. Must be able to exercise with children on the playground and in the classroom.

E. Must be able physically and mentally to react immediately to unexpected and emergency circumstances.

F. Must be able to stoop and bend to a young child's level.

IV.   Job Requirements

A. Must support and implement the Kids-R-Ours educational philosophy.

B. Must provide a positive, loving, and nurturing environment for children.

C. Must display respect for children and adults.

D. Must maintain classroom environment in a neat and inviting manner.

E. Must maintain order and discipline in the classroom.

F. Must follow prescribed administrative procedures.

G. Must follow cleanliness procedures.

Adopted January, YR-6

KIDS-R-OURS, INC.

Policy On Written Communications To Parents

All written announcements, bulletins, and newsletters must be approved by the director before being sent out to parents. This policy does not apply to notes written to individual parents concerning their particular child.

Adopted January, YR-10

KIDS-R-OURS, INC.

<u>Non-Discrimination Policy</u>

It is the policy of Kids-R-Ours, Inc., to prohibit discrimination in employment and in the provision of services on the basis of race, religion, sex, age, marital status, national origin, and ancestry. Kids-R-Ours, Inc., adheres to all State and Federal laws prohibiting discrimination in the workplace and in places of public accommodation.

Adopted January, YR-5

KIDS-R-OURS, INC.

100 Center Street
Nita City, Nita 39396
(333) 234-5678

August 31, YR-2

Dear Parents,

I am writing to tell you that I will no longer be the head teacher in the two year old class. Leona has demoted me to assistant teacher in the four year old class.

Leona feels it would be safer if I worked with the older children since I have a seizure disorder. I disagree with this. I would never jeopardize the safety of the children. However, I have no choice but to accept Leona's decision.

I wanted you to know that I have really enjoyed working with your children, and I will miss them a lot. I look forward to working with them in a few years when they reach the four year old class.

Sincerely,

Jean Jones

Jean Jones

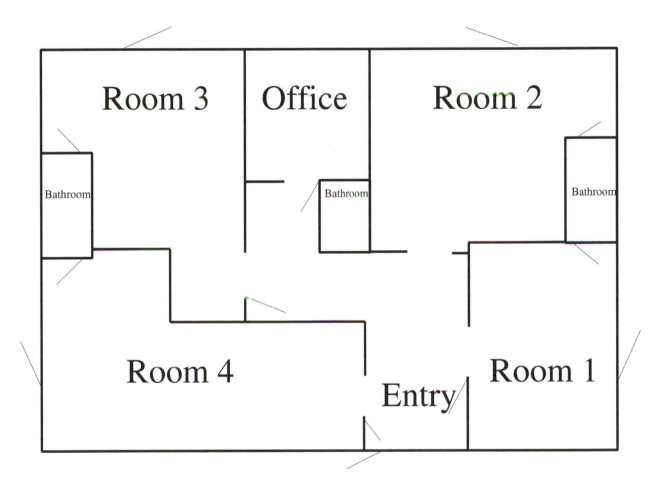

Room 3   Office   Room 2

Bathroom   Bathroom   Bathroom

Room 4   Room 1

Entry

N
↑
↓
S

Nita Agency Regulations § 100-10-1

Day Care Center Staffing Ratios: Every day care center operating in the State of Nita must at all times maintain staff-to-child ratios as follows:

(a)   For children aged 36 months or less, one staff member to four children.

(b)   For children older than 36 months, one staff member to every eight children.

KIDS-R-OURS-INC.
YR-2 BUDGET

INCOME

1.	Payments from families		$ 840,000.00
		TOTAL	$ 840,000.00

EXPENDITURES

1.	Salaries		$ 580,000.00
2.	Benefits		120,000.00
3.	Rent		45,000.00
4.	Equipment and supplies, including van		45,000.00
5.	Utilities		30,000.00
6.	Insurance		20,000.00
		TOTAL	$ 840,000.00

NITA NEUROLOGICAL GROUP, INC.

750 Monroe Avenue
Nita City, Nita 39396
(333) 745-7457

August 27, YR-2

Re: Jean Jones

To Whom It May Concern:

Jean's seizure condition is substantially controlled with medication. However, it is not possible to say that she could expect to be seizure free in the immediate future.

I believe that any possible danger to children resulting from Jean's medical condition could be eliminated if she does not lift or carry children or stay alone with them for more than a few minutes at a time.

I hope this letter addresses your concerns. If you have additional questions, please contact me.

P.R. Gray, M.D.

JEAN P. JONES
100 Runner Road
Nita City, Nita 39396
(333) 232-4567

*Experience*_____

Bright Horizons Day Care Center	Central City, Nita
Assistant Teacher	11/YR-3 to 5/YR-2

- Supervised, planned, and led children's activities, both inside and outside. Read to children and organized snack time.

Oakwood Community School	Central City, Nita
Assistant Teacher	6/YR-3 to 8/YR-3

- Supervised planned activities, indoor and outdoor play, and field trips. Read to children and set out snacks.

Nita Day Camp	Nita City, Nita
Camp Counselor	6/YR-4 to 8/YR-4

- Supervised camp activities, swimming, crafts, and lunch.

*Education*_____

Lancaster College	Central City, Nita
Associate's Degree	9/YR-5 to 6/YR-3
Early Childhood Education	

*Internships*_____

Children's House Day Care	Central City, Nita
Teacher's Aide	9/YR-4 to 5/YR-3

- Helped supervise play activities and lunch.

Central City Day Care	Central City, Nita
Teacher's Aide	1/YR-4 to 5/YR-4

- Helped supervise play activities and lunch.

Lancaster College Day Care	Central City, Nita
Teacher's Aide	9/YR-5 to 12/YR-5

- Played games with children, read books, and helped with snacks.

*References*_____

Available upon request

STATE OF NITA
COMMISSION ON HUMAN RIGHTS AND OPPORTUNITIES

AFFIDAVIT OF ILLEGAL DISCRIMINATORY PRACTICE

Date: ___July 14, YR-3_____   Case No.: ___9212345_____

My name is ___Garrett Griswold_____

and I reside ___22 Robbins Street, Nita City, Nita 39396_____

The respondent is ___Kids-R-Ours, Inc._____

who business address is ___100 Center Street, Nita City, Nita 39396_____

I was notified on ___June 4_____, _YR-3_, and

(**x**) discharged ( ) not hired/not promoted
( ) suspended ( ) not rented a dwelling
( ) demoted   ( ) denied sale of a dwelling
( ) retaliated against   ( ) constructively discharged
( ) placed on probation   ( ) warned
( ) earning a different rate of pay   ( ) given a poor evaluation
( ) denied union representation   ( ) denied a raise
( ) less trained ( ) denied an office
( ) harassed

on ___June 4_____, _YR-3_, and believe that my

( ) race   (**x**) mental retardation
( ) color   ( ) religious creed
( ) sex   ( ) familial status
( ) pregnancy ( ) sexual orientation
( ) ancestry   (**x**) mental disorder
( ) age   ( ) alienage
( ) religion   ( ) learning disability
( ) national origin   ( ) physical disability
( ) marital status   ( ) creed

was in part a factor in this action.

I provide the following particulars:

1. My name is Garrett Griswold and I reside at 22 Robbins Road, Nita City, Nita 39396.

2. The respondent is Kids-R-Ours, Inc., whose business address is 100 Center Street, Nita City, Nita 39396.

3. The respondent employs more than 25 people.

4. I have mental retardation (borderline) caused by Down Syndrome.

5. On or about January 13, YR-3, I began employment with the respondent as a janitor at an hourly wage of $5.50. My work schedule was Mondays through Fridays, 12:00 through 5:00 p.m.

6. On or about June 4, YR-3, the respondent's director, Leona Odell, fired me without warning.

7. I believe that the respondent fired me because of my mental retardation because:

   a. When I asked Ms. Odell why she was firing me, she said she had received complaints from several parents that I was "upsetting" their children.

   b. Ms. Odell also said my janitorial work had been poor; however, neither she nor anyone else at Kids-R-Ours had ever said anything negative to me about my job performance before.

   c. Upon information and belief, I was the only employee of the respondent with any type of mental or physical disability.

I therefore request that the Nita Commission on Human Rights and Opportunities investigate my complaint, secure for me my rights as guaranteed by state and federal law, and secure for me any remedy to which I may be entitled.

___Garrett Griswold___, being duly sworn, states that he is the complainant herein; that he has read the foregoing complaint and knows the content hereof; and that the same is true of his own knowledge or belief.

Dated at _Nita City, Nita_, this _14th_ day of _July_, _YR-3_.

Garrett Griswold
Complainant's signature

Subscribed and sworn to before me this _14th_ day of _July_, _YR-3_.

Marsha Ball
Notary Public
My commission expires: 12/14/YR-0

1234 Cedar Street
Nita City, Nita 39396

February 25, YR-2

Leona Odell, Director
Kids-R-Ours, Inc.
100 Center Street
Nita City, Nita 39396

Re: Garrett Griswold vs. Kids-R-Ours, Inc.
        Case No. 9212345

Dear Ms. Odell:

This will confirm that, following the Commission's finding of probable cause to believe that discrimination had occurred, a conciliation conference was held on January 21, YR-2, at which the parties agreed to a voluntary resolution of this matter. Accordingly, the above-referenced complaint has been withdrawn by the complainant.

The Commission's files in this matter will now be closed.

Please contact the undersigned if any further information is needed.

Very truly yours,

J. Ring
Investigator

B. Spork
Regional Manager

cc: Garrett Griswold

KIDS-R-OURS, INC.

<u>Organizational Chart</u>

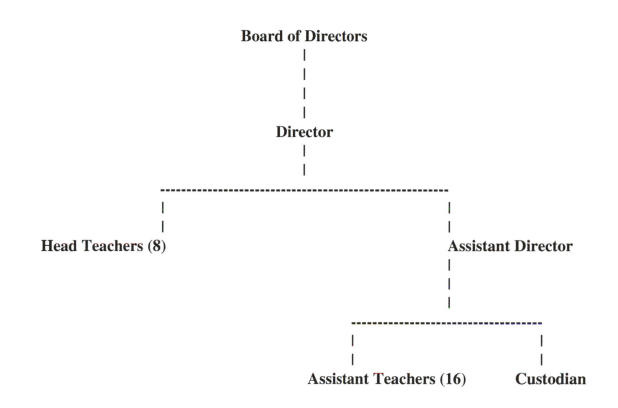

Board of Directors

Director

Head Teachers (8)

Assistant Director

Assistant Teachers (16)　　　**Custodian**

Jones v. Kids-R-Ours

STATE OF NITA	:	SUPERIOR COURT
v.	:	DISTRICT OF NITA CITY
JOYCE STAPLES	:	AT NITA CITY
	:	APRIL 15, YR-1

CERTIFIED RECORD OF JUDGMENT

Notice is hereby given that on September 4, YR-9, the above-named defendant, Joyce Staples, was convicted of the crime of possession of cocaine in violation of Nita Gen. Stat. § 18a-134(a) and sentenced to two years probation. Possession of cocaine is a Class C felony punishable by up to 5 years imprisonment.

I hereby certify accordingly under seal.

John Mills
Deputy Clerk

OFFICIAL SEAL

NITA NEUROLOGICAL GROUP, INC.

750 Monroe Avenue
Nita City, Nita 39396
(333) 745-7457

February 15, YR-1

Statement: Jean Jones

Date	Service	Fee
9/14/YR-2	Office visit Neurological examination	$ 150.00
1/11/YR-1	Office visit Neurological examination	$ 150.00
	TOTAL	$ 300.00

O. HENRY, PH.D.

Licensed Psychologist
100 Prospect Street
Nita City, Nita 39396
(333) 879-3250

February 15, YR-1

Statement: Jean Jones

For professional services from September 5, YR-2, through February 15, YR-1.

20 sessions @ $100 . . . . $2,000

DWT PHARMACY

26 Cottage Grove Road
Nita City, Nita 39396
(333) 987-0235

February 15, YR-1

RECORD OF PURCHASES

PREPARED FOR:

Jean Jones
100 Runner Road
Nita City, Nita 39396

Date	Medication	Amount	Dosage	Cost
9/15/YR-2	Dilantin	60	100 mg.	$75.00
	Depakote	120	250 mg.	100.00
10/15/YR-2	Dilantin	60	100 mg.	75.00
	Depakote	120	250 mg.	100.00
11/15/YR-2	Dilantin	60	100 mg.	75.00
	Depakote	120	250 mg.	100.00
12/15/YR-2	Dilantin	60	100 mg.	75.00
	Depakote	120	250 mg.	100.00
1/15/YR-1	Dilantin	60	100 mg.	75.00
	Depakote	120	250 mg.	100.00
2/15/YR-1	Dilantin	60	100 mg.	75.00
	Depakote	120	250 mg.	100.00
			TOTAL	$ 1,050.00

JURY INSTRUCTIONS

1.   <u>Introduction; Functions of Judge and Jury</u>: Ladies and gentlemen, I will now instruct you on the law governing this case.

      The judge and jury have separate functions. It is my duty to state the rules of law that govern this case; it is your duty to decide the facts. What I say about the law is binding on you. Deciding the facts, however, is entirely and exclusively up to you. Nothing that I or any of the lawyers say about the facts is binding upon you.

2.   <u>Verdict to Be Unanimous and Based Solely on the Evidence</u>: Your verdict must be unanimous. It must be based solely upon the evidence presented in this courtroom today. You should not be influenced by sympathy for, or prejudice against, either of the parties.

3.   <u>Credibility of Witnesses</u>: You alone must determine the credibility of witnesses and the weight to give to their testimony. In evaluating credibility, you should use your good, ordinary common sense as members of the community. Use the same considerations that you apply in everyday life when questions of truth and credibility arise. Consider, for example, any possible bias or prejudice a witness may have; his or her interest, or lack of interest, in the outcome of the trial; and his or her ability to observe facts correctly, and to remember and relate them truly and accurately.

      Obviously, no fact should be determined merely by the number of witnesses testifying for or against it. It is quality, rather than quantity, of testimony that controls.

      If you believe that a witness has testified falsely in one regard, this doesn't necessarily mean that you should disbelieve everything that witness said. Whether to believe all, some or none of a witness' testimony is for you and you alone to decide using your knowledge of and experience with human nature.

4.   <u>Burden of Proof, in General</u>: The Plaintiff, Jean Jones, has the burden of proof in this case, as does the plaintiff in all civil cases. This means that the Plaintiff must prove that her version of the facts is true. The Defendant, Kids-R-Ours, is not required to disprove the Plaintiff's case.

      Unfortunately, however, things are slightly more complicated than that. For although the Plaintiff has the initial burden of proof, the Defendant may also have the burden of proving certain things called "affirmative defenses." It works like this: If you decide that the Plaintiff satisfied her burden of proof on a particular claim, then you will have to decide whether the Defendant proved its affirmative defenses with regard to that claim. If, however, you decide that the Plaintiff did not satisfy her burden of proof, then you don't even need to consider the affirmative defenses. I think this will make somewhat more sense when I get to the specifics of this case, which I will do in a moment.

5.   Burden of Proof: Fair Preponderance of the Evidence Standard: Before I get to that, I need to explain the standard of proof in this case. When I say that the Plaintiff or the Defendant must prove something to you, I mean that they must demonstrate that it is more likely than not true. This is called the "fair preponderance of evidence" standard.

Many of you are probably familiar with the term, "proof beyond a reasonable doubt." That is the standard that applies in criminal cases. It does <u>not</u> apply here, and you should put it out of your minds entirely. No one in this case is required to prove anything beyond a reasonable doubt.

To apply the fair preponderance of evidence standard, you must take all the evidence you have heard, weigh and balance it, and decide whether the evidence tips in favor of the party who has the burden of proof on that issue -- even if ever so slightly. If it does, that party has satisfied the burden of proof on that issue. If it does not, the party has not satisfied the burden. If the evidence is so evenly balanced that it does not tip one way or the other, then the party with the burden of proof on that issue also has not satisfied the burden.

6.   The Plaintiff's Claims: The Plaintiff in this case, Jean Jones, claims that the Defendant, Kids-R-Ours, violated a federal civil rights law known as the Americans with Disabilities Act, or ADA. The relevant portion of this law states that an employer covered by the ADA may not discriminate against a person with a disability who is able to perform the essential functions of the job with or without reasonable accommodation.

The Plaintiff claims that the Defendant violated the ADA in two different ways. First, the Plaintiff claims that the Defendant discriminated against her by demoting or reassigning her to the position of assistant teacher in the four year old classroom. Second, the Plaintiff claims that the Defendant discriminated by firing her because of her disability.

In this case, the Defendant has admitted that it is covered by the ADA. The Defendant has also admitted that the Plaintiff is a person with a disability as defined by the ADA. The Defendant has denied, however, that it in any way discriminated against the Plaintiff in violation of the ADA.

[Judge: Please give the following instruction only if appropriate:] You have heard conflicting testimony about whether or not the Plaintiff disclosed her disability to Leona Odell at her job interview. You should know that the ADA does <u>not</u> require that a job applicant disclose her disability to a prospective employer. At the same time, an employer may not ask a job applicant whether she in fact has a disability. The employer may only ask the applicant about her ability to perform the specific tasks required in the job.

7.   Demotion / Reassignment Claim: Let's first turn to the Plaintiff's claim that the Defendant discriminated against her by demoting or reassigning her to the position of assistant teacher in the four year old classroom. In order to prevail on this claim, the Plaintiff must prove that she was capable of performing the essential functions of her job as head teacher of two year olds with or without reasonable accommodation.

The term "essential functions" means fundamental job duties. It does not include marginal or peripheral duties. Factors you may consider in determining whether a function is essential include, but are not limited to: the written job description; the employer's judgment as to which functions are essential; and the work experience of other employees in that job.

The term "reasonable accommodation" means reasonable adjustments to the way in which a job is usually performed that enable a person with a disability to perform the essential functions of a job. Examples of accommodations include, but are not limited to, job restructuring and physical modification of the workplace.

You must decide, then, whether the Plaintiff satisfied her burden of proving that she was capable of performing the essential functions of her job as head teacher of two year olds with or without reasonable accommodation. If she failed to prove this, your verdict must be for the Defendant on this particular claim. If, however, the Plaintiff did prove this to you, you must go on to consider the two affirmative defenses that the Defendant has raised with regard to this claim.

The Defendant's first affirmative defense is that to accommodate the plaintiff's disability in the two year old classroom would have imposed an "undue hardship" on the Defendant. The ADA does not require that an employer make an accommodation that would impose an undue hardship on it. An undue hardship means significant difficulty or expense given an employer's financial, administrative, and staff resources.

The Defendant's second affirmative defense is that the Plaintiff's disability posed a direct threat to the health or safety of other individuals in the two year old classroom. The term "direct threat" means a significant risk of harm to the health or safety of others that cannot be eliminated or reduced by reasonable accommodation. Factors you may consider in determining whether the Plaintiff posed a direct threat include, but are not limited to: the duration of the risk; the nature and severity of the potential harm; and the likelihood that the potential harm would have occurred.

Remember, when it comes to affirmative defenses, the burden of proof is on the Defendant. If you decide that the Defendant proved either of these two affirmative defenses, your verdict should be in favor of the Defendant on this claim. If, however, you decide that the Defendant did not prove either of these affirmative defenses, your verdict should be for the Plaintiff. (This assumes, of course, that you previously decided that the Plaintiff proved she was capable of performing the essential functions of her job as head teacher of two year olds with or without reasonable accommodation.)

8.   Dismissal Claim: Now let's turn to the Plaintiff's claim that the Defendant discriminated against her by firing her. The issue here is not whether the Plaintiff was capable of performing the essential functions of the job as assistant teacher in the four year old classroom with or without reasonable accommodation. The Defendant basically conceded this by reassigning the Plaintiff to that position in the first place. Rather, the issue here is the Defendant's motivation for firing the Plaintiff from that position.

In order to prevail on this claim, the Plaintiff must prove that her disability was at least one motivating factor in the Defendant's decision to fire her. To do this, the Plaintiff must demonstrate that the Defendant's stated reason for firing her -- insubordination -- was not the real reason, or at least not the whole reason, that she was fired. If the Plaintiff proves this by a fair preponderance of the evidence, then the law allows you to infer that her disability was a motivating factor in the Defendant's actions. You don't have to infer this but you may.

If you decide that the Plaintiff did <u>not</u> prove that her disability was a motivating factor in the Defendant's decision to fire her, your verdict must be for the Defendant on this claim. If, however, you find that the Plaintiff <u>did</u> prove that her disability was a factor, you must go on to consider the affirmative defense that the Defendant has raised on this claim.

The Defendant's affirmative defense to this claim is that it would have made the same decision to fire the Plaintiff even if she did not have a disability. In other words, even if the Plaintiff's disability was a motivating factor, it didn't affect the outcome because the Defendant would have fired a person without a disability under the same or similar circumstances.

If you decide that the Defendant <u>did</u> prove that it would have made the same decision to fire the plaintiff even if she did not have a disability, your verdict should be in favor of the Defendant on this claim. If you decide that the defendant did <u>not</u> prove this affirmative defense, your verdict should be in favor of the Plaintiff on this claim.

9.   <u>Direct and Circumstantial Evidence</u>: Now I want to say a word about direct and circumstantial evidence, since these concepts will necessarily play a role in your consideration of whether the Defendant discriminated against the Plaintiff by firing her.

Direct evidence is often called "eyewitness" evidence. To use an example, suppose that you look out the window and see rain falling. That is direct, eyewitness evidence that it is raining.

Circumstantial evidence is another word for "indirect" evidence. It is evidence of one fact or set of facts from which another fact can be inferred. To use the same example, suppose that your friend comes into the house dripping wet. From that fact you can infer that it is raining outside. This is an example of circumstantial evidence. For your purposes, there is no legal difference between direct and circumstantial evidence. Both are legitimate forms of evidence.

In this case, the Plaintiff's claim that her disability was a motivating factor in the Defendant's decision to fire her is based solely upon circumstantial evidence. So is the Defendant's affirmative defense to this claim (that the Defendant would have taken the same action even if the Plaintiff had no disability). There is no direct evidence for either of these propositions. You must decide whether the circumstantial evidence supports the inferences suggested by the parties. Remember that the Plaintiff must convince you to draw the inference she wants by a fair preponderance of the evidence, and the Defendant must do the same with respect to its affirmative defense.

11.   Employment at Will: One thing you must keep in mind is that the Plaintiff was a so-called "at-will" employee. This means that the Defendant was entitled to fire her for any reason whatsoever, so long as it was not an illegal reason like disability discrimination. The issue, then, is not whether the Defendant acted fairly or unfairly in discharging the plaintiff; it is whether the Defendant fired her because of her disability.

12.   Bifurcation: You may have noticed that the Plaintiff and her lawyers have not said anything about any economic losses or other damages she may have suffered. That is because, in this trial, you will only be deciding whether the Defendant violated the Americans with Disabilities Act. If you decide that the Defendant did violate the law, there will be a second trial to determine the Plaintiff's damages, if any. (Don't worry; you won't have to stick around for it!) In your deliberations today, you must disregard any harm Jean Jones may have suffered.

13.   Conclusion; Election of Foreperson: Let me remind you once again that your consideration of this case should be based solely on the evidence presented and the instructions I have given. The parties to this action are entitled to have a calm, careful, conscientious appraisal of the issues presented to you. Sympathy, bias or prejudice should not have the slightest influence upon you in reaching your verdict. I am sure that you will live up to your oath and will exclude these considerations.

I thank you for your time and patience. Once this courtroom is cleared, you should stay here and proceed with your deliberations. One of the first things you must do when the rest of us leave the courtroom is to elect one member of the jury as the foreperson. That person will preside over the deliberations, fill out the verdict form, and speak for you here in open court. Consider one another's opinions but reach your own decisions. Remember that a unanimous verdict is required. Please inform the marshal here when your verdict is ready. If you have any questions or want any of my instructions clarified as you deliberate, please let the marshal know.

This court now stands in recess.

UNITED STATES DISTRICT COURT
DISTRICT OF NITA

JEAN JONES,   :   CIVIL NO. N-93-96369 (ABC)
    Plaintiff,   :

v.   :

KIDS-R-OURS, INC.,   :
    Defendant   :

GENERAL JURY VERDICT

We, the jury, unanimously decide as follows:

The Defendant **DID / DID NOT** [please circle one] discriminate against the Plaintiff, in violation of the Americans with Disabilities Act, by demoting or reassigning her to the position of assistant teacher in the four year old classroom.

The Defendant **DID / DID NOT** [please circle one] discriminate against the Plaintiff, in violation of the Americans with Disabilities Act, by firing her.

This is our verdict, and we all agree on it.

_____

[Foreperson please sign here]

CPSIA information can be obtained
at www.ICGtesting.com
Printed in the USA
FFHW012211170119
50204287-55164FF